101 Ways to get your Child to Read

Patience Thomson

with a foreword by

Michael Morpurgo

Barrington Stoke Ltd

First published in 2009 in Great Britain by
Barrington Stoke Ltd
18 Walker Street, Edinburgh, EH3 7LP

www.barringtonstoke.co.uk

ISBN: 978-1-84299-671-3

Printed in Great Britain by CPI Bookmarque Ltd

Contents

About the Author

Patience Thomson is a writer, a lecturer and an expert on reading. She was Principal of Fairley House, a school for dyslexic children. Ten years ago she co-founded Barrington Stoke, a company that publishes books for reluctant readers. She is the mother and grandmother of dyslexic children.

Acknowledgements

I would like to thank Kate Paice, Linda McQueen, Jane Page, Alex Tait, Bernadette McLean, Sophie Wells, my husband David and my son Hugh for all the advice and support they have given me in writing this book.

I dedicate this book to all my pupils, with grateful thanks for all they taught me.

Patience Thomson

Foreword

by Michael Morpurgo

It's sometime in 1947. Picture a small boy aged about four, sitting up in bed, short sticky-up hair, striped pyjamas and a very restless mind. He's waiting for something, for his mother to come and read him a story. He's washed his hands and face, and scrubbed behind his ears, and he's brushed his teeth. He's done this because he knows he won't get a story unless he has. She'll check. She comes in and sits down on the bed.

It's a great moment, the best moment. Mum all to myself for a while, and a story. "'Elephant's Child' or 'Jumblies'?" she asks me.

"'Elephant's Child'," I tell her, because it's longer. I want her to stay longer. I lie back on my pillow, pull the sheet up to my chin, and watch her. I love to watch her because I know I'll be seeing the story in her face as she tells it. That's because she lives the story, and loves the story as she tells it.

She opens the book. "Here we go," she says. "'In the High and Far-Off Times, the

Elephant, O Best Beloved, had no trunk. He had only a blackish, bulgy nose, as big as a boot, that he could wriggle about from side to side; but he couldn't pick up things with it...'"

And off I go with the Elephant's Child, down to the "great grey-green, greasy Limpopo river", where his curiosity gets him into all sorts of difficulties with a certain crocodile who is just waiting to grab him by his nose.

I know the story almost word for word, love the sheer fun of it, and the excitement of it. I never want it to end. But of course it does end, in the end! She turns out the light, gives me a kiss and leaves the door ajar as I like it. I am left with just the scent of her face powder, and with Kipling's story of the Elephant's Child deep in my head.

I was so lucky. I had a mother who loved to read me stories and poems. And that's the point. She loved doing it. I could tell that by the way she read it. She was enjoying the story as much as I was. The story was the link between us. In that little room there was her, me and the story. They were moments that I kept for always, and maybe she did too. She read beautifully, so that I could hear the music in the words, the rhythms in the sentences.

Then I went off to school, where I discovered all too soon that the words I had loved, and the stories I had loved, were simply used by teachers to test me on my spelling and punctuation and understanding. This turned me off, and for years my love of stories and poems lay sleeping. Then as a teacher I found myself in front of 36 year 6 children. I found out the only way to have them all involved and focused was a good story. I read only the stories I loved, and read them with a passion as my mother had. Then one day I dared to make up one of my own. I lived that story as I told it, and they believed it with me. They loved it. They became great readers, and great writers too.

Mr Aesop's tales all had a moral. So why not follow his good example? If as a parent or teacher you read to a child and make it a special moment, if you read because you love it, then the child will catch that love like a falling star, and put it in his pocket for life. He'll store it up in his heart. The star may fade, almost lose its light some-

times, but it will always be there. You will
have given that child one of the greatest
gifts we can pass on, the joy of reading.

Michael Morpurgo

Michael Morpurgo OBE worked as a
teacher before becoming a full-time writer.
Michael was Children's Laureate 2003–05,
and has won many prizes for his books
including the Whitbread Prize, the Smarties
Prize and the Children's Book Award. He
and his wife run the charity Farms For City
Children (FFCC), which brings young
children from towns to live and work in
the countryside.

Introduction

I have worked for many years with the parents of children who find it hard to learn to read. Many parents want questions answered. Why does my child find reading so hard? Will he learn in the end? What can I do to help? How can I change his negative attitude?

There is such a lot parents can do to help, with support and encouragement. You don't have to be a confident reader yourself. Many of you will have thought of good ideas, but no parent can think of everything. So it makes sense to share the tips that have helped others.

The tips in this book have been well tested by parents and pupils, and by professionals in the field. They can work for you.

Just as there is a different pattern to the difficulties of each individual child, so there is a range of solutions. Choose which tips are most useful for you! If you want to know more, use the Useful Addresses section at the back of the book to find organisations that can give you more help and advice.

I have tried to leave out jargon and anything that was too technical or just plain boring. I have included lots of true stories, to show that you are not alone.

. This is the book I would love to have given to the parents I have counselled over the years. This is the book that would have saved me so much grief if I had read it when my own nine-year-old son could not read or write.

Why is it important to learn to read?

Knowing how to read for yourself is the single most important thing in life, in my opinion. It's like learning to fly on your own and you need never be bored ever again. Every journey is better if you have a paperback in your pocket; each night (and therefore bedtime) becomes madly attractive knowing that your book is waiting for you.

And learning to read is a struggle that will only happen once, like learning to swim or ride a bike. Once reading is mastered, the world opens up.

Joanna Lumley

I have years of experience of teaching children to read. I was Principal of Fairley House, a school in London for dyslexic children, and later I co-founded Barrington Stoke, a company that publishes books for reluctant readers. Parents have sent me a lot of letters over the years. They have told me what a big difference reading has made to their children's lives. Here are just three of these letters:

"Today [my son is] an enthusiastic, indeed avid reader who is much more confident [and] in touch with people around him."

"I just can't believe it!!! Our dyslexic grandson, Dominic, has just finished reading two books – this really is a breakthrough as he read them so quickly and without encouragement. His mother had to turn his bedroom light off at 1 am. He just wouldn't put the book down. He is now heading into year 6 and we feel his self-esteem has been raised. Hopefully this will help him through this next difficult year before he transfers to secondary school."

"My son is 14 and has learning difficulties. He is now sitting down and reading with enjoyment for the first time in his life. It has opened up a whole new world for him."

Every single child will benefit from reading. Every child will be more confident if he or she learns to read well. Every child can find a whole new world of interest, adventure, learning and fun, just by opening a book. And every child must have the chance to learn to read, because reading changes lives.

You probably picked up this book because you know how important reading is these days. Reading can give a child so much joy. But if a child never learns to read, it can affect his or her whole life.

If children are poor readers, they will be more likely to fall behind at school. Homework, tests and exams will be much harder. Other children may call them names and say they're stupid.

Some children get used to failing. They may even choose to fail because it's easier that way. They may decide they are stupid, since everyone else thinks so. They may stop trying. They may feel frustrated and bored. They may muck about and get in trouble, or even bunk off school.

It's hard to get good exam results when reading is a struggle. And when you leave school, what do you do? More than 98 per cent of jobs in Britain today need reading skills.

Reading is part of everyday life. You need to read to get a driving licence, use the internet, shop, book a holiday, fill in forms, take the right medicine, order food in a cafe, catch the bus in the right direction, set up a DVD player and find out what's on TV.

If you have problems reading, everything in life is harder. If you learn to love reading, you don't miss out – and you can have so much fun!

Helping your child to read well can be the most important thing you ever do for him or her.

Helping children to read

Some children learn to read when they are very young with almost no help at all. They just seem to pick it up naturally. Some people can't even remember a time when they didn't know how to read. They are the lucky ones.

Others learn to read at school. They remember later how exciting it was when the words on the page suddenly began to make sense.

And some children have the same help and yet do not seem able to learn. They are often as clever as the others. They want to learn to read. But for a lot of different reasons it just doesn't happen.

It is not the teacher's fault. It is not the parents' fault. And most of all, it is not the child's fault.

Maybe these children have problems such as dyslexia. Maybe they have been off sick and have missed a lot of school.

Some children don't like reading because it's hard work, or they're afraid to try and fail. Maybe their parents and friends don't read. Maybe TV is just more fun!

Boys are more likely to have reading problems, though plenty of girls struggle too.

Why do girls have fewer problems? It may be to do with how we evolved. Women spent more time together looking after the children, so they talked more. Their brains developed to be good with the spoken word. Now, in our modern world, they are wired up better to deal with the written word too.

It can be very hard for a parent to help. Perhaps you aren't a confident reader yourself. Perhaps you want to help, but you don't have time. Perhaps your child seems to hate books, or has given up trying to read, and you don't know what to do.

Getting started can be hard, and that's what this book is all about.

The good news

You only have to learn to read once. Even if children learn slowly, with the right help they will get there. The important thing is that they are making progress.

That's where parents come in. You are the only people who can give constant support over the years. And there is such a lot you can do.

- You can help your child to get started on letters (**Chapter One, Starting to Read**, p.11).

- You can learn how your child's mind works, so that you can find the best way to help (**Chapter Two, How Does My Child's Mind Work?**, p.31).

- You can find out what's stopping your child from reading, and look for ways round it (**Chapter Three, Types of Reading Problem**, p.46).

- You can change your child's attitude to reading. It is a great help to have books in the house, which you can get from a library, supermarket, charity shop or bookshop. Looking through picture books with your young child is a fun and easy way to start. It's important for you or another adult to read books to your child from a young age. Maybe you can learn to love books together! (**Chapter Four, Changing Attitudes**, p.62).

- Your child will need support from you, both before starting school and right through his or her school career. But children's needs change as they get older and you will need to find out what they are. You can also support your child a lot by showing him or her how to get organised, if he or she finds that difficult (**Chapter Five, Tots to Teens**, p.77).

- You can make sure that your child has the right things to read, like books and magazines that he or she really enjoys. (**Chapter Six, Choosing the Right Book**, p.94).

- Some parents might like to brush up their own reading skills (**Chapter Seven, Adults and Reading**, p.116).

- There are also lots of contact details and links in **Useful Addresses**, p.132. You can find some really good advice for parents from the National Literacy Trust (www.literacytrust.org.uk /familyreading/parents). NIACE provides great support for parents who want to improve their own reading and help their children (www.niace.org.uk).

You don't need to read the whole of this book from start to end – it's up to you to decide what you need to know!

On the way you will find 101 tips for you to pick and choose from. They won't all work for everyone – every parent and every child is different! But some of it will be perfect for you and your child. Some of the advice is aimed at children with Specific Learning Difficulties, lots of it is great for all children. There is advice for all parents, including those who are struggling with reading themselves. See pages 70–2 and Chapter Seven if you find reading difficult.

This book will give you the help you need to give your child the best possible start in life. Good luck – and have fun!

Chapter One

Starting to Read – the basics

To make this chapter easier to read, I will use "he" or "him" to refer to your child. The tips and advice work for boys and girls!

The first part of this chapter is for you if your child missed out when the rest of the class learned to read. The other children and the teacher have moved on but he's still struggling with letters or simple words. Here are some ways to help him learn his letters in the time you have together on evenings, weekends and holidays.

Ask the school what they are doing for him. He might be getting special help. But it will be much better if you can work with him at home. Chat to his teacher. If your child is still learning to read at school, keep in touch with the teacher and find if there are ways you can help with what he's learning in class. Then you will be sure that he's learning by one method only, and won't get confused.

However, lots of the tips and games suggested in this chapter will work with any method of learning to read!

There are lots of ways to teach a child to read, and most of them are not right or wrong. One method doesn't suit every child.

Here are some ideas for what you can do if your child is still finding it hard to learn his letters. These ideas have three big plus points.

- They seem to work well for all children.
- They are easy for parents to follow.
- They are not likely to muddle a child who is being taught by a different method at school

If your child hasn't begun to read yet, these methods will help him to learn the basics. But first we must be clear what reading is all about. And you must begin right at the very beginning.

Step 1: Starting on letters

The basic facts about letters

The first thing a child must know about when he is learning to read are the shapes and sounds of all the letters used in the English language. Then he can put them together and find out what each word says.

- Every letter has a different **shape**. To read, we have to tell one letter from another: **d** and **o** and **g** do not look the same.

- There are also **big** (**capital**) and little letters, **D** and **d**. Don't confuse things by bringing that up yet. Stick to the small **a**, **b** and **c**.

- Letters have different **sounds**. You need to know which sounds letters make to work out what each letter in a word is saying: **d-o-g**.

- Each letter also has a **name**. D is called "dee". We use this when we go through the alphabet, "a-b-c", or spell out a word, "h-o-t". Leave these names for when your child has really got started.

Your child may use a 'phonics' programme at school, which will include this method of sounding out letters. Your child's school can tell you more about how they use phonics.

TIP 1 To remember them better, your child may like to give the letters nicknames like "Sammy Snake" for S.

He may have done this at school and be able to tell you what the nicknames are. If he can't remember, make up some new ones.

When I taught young men in prison to read, they chose "Busty Brenda" for B and "Sexy Susie" for S. You can guess what they had for F.

Vowels and consonants

Next, you need to teach your child which letters are vowels (**a**, **e**, **i**, **o**, **u** and sometimes **y**) and which are consonants.

TIP 2 Jam sandwiches.

I first got the basic idea of making "jam sandwiches" in the 1970s from a teacher and have been developing the idea ever since.

- Buy a set of plastic or wooden letters.
- Also buy two small pots of paint, one red, and one yellow. (Enamel modelling paint is best because it sticks to plastic or wood.)
- Now paint the letters red and yellow. Get your child to help. Read on before starting.

14

- Five letters must be red – **a**, **e**, **i**, **o**, and **u**. These are called the vowels. One more letter, **y**, is sometimes a consonant (like in "yes") and sometimes a vowel (like in "try") so paint it half red. The vowels are the jam in your word sandwiches. You can't have a word without at least one vowel in it – just as you can't have a sandwich without a filling.
- Now paint all the other letters yellow – they are the bread for your sandwiches. All these other letters are consonants. Don't forget to paint some yellow on the **y** to show it's sometimes a consonant.
- As you work at painting the letters, find out if your child knows any of their sounds or shapes. Don't waste time teaching him anything he knows already!

If it's too difficult getting plastic letters, you can do this with cards and write on them with red and yellow felt pen, but it doesn't work quite as well, because the child will learn faster if he can "feel" the shape of the letters.

Adding letters one by one

You're ready to get going. Remember, at this early stage always say the sound of the letter, **b**, and not its name ("bee"). Otherwise your child will get confused.

TIP 3 Start with the child's own name. Suppose it's Sam. Then **s** is his letter. Let him feel its shape. Trace it on his hand with your finger. Let him say its sound. Tell him it belongs to him. Now there are only 25 more letters left to learn!

TIP 4 Here are two more easy ones. Mum's letter is **m** and Dad's letter is **d**. Use the names of parents, carers, brothers, sisters and friends to extend the range of letters.

TIP 5 Get him to shut his eyes. Give him plastic letters of very different shapes – **s** and **k** and **m**. Get him to tell you which is which just by feeling them.

TIP 6 Write a big letter on his back with your finger. Can he tell you what it is? Then get him to write a letter on your back for you to guess. Tell him, "Wow, we're getting somewhere!"

TIP 7 Think of the food he likes best and find its letter. Pringles, pasta and pizza all share a first letter.

TIP 8 Get him to listen carefully to the first sound in a word and ask him to say what it is. Lion starts with **l** and elephant with **e**. Play guessing games. "I spy with my little eye something beginning with **b**..."

TIP 9 Pick out a letter and try to find an animal that starts with that letter. Remember to use the sound of the letter, not the name. ("I'm thinking of a wild animal that begins with a **t**. "Tiger!" "Well done! It's your turn now.")

TIP 10 Make letters together out of Plasticine so he can feel their shape.

Step 2: Starting on words

Next, your child needs to know that you can put letters together to make a word and that a word has a meaning. So **d-o-g** becomes a furry animal, which barks and wags its tail.

You can begin with very simple three-letter words. If the child has learnt the sound of all the letters, he will be able to work most of these simple words out.

At this stage it all gets rather exciting because you put words together into sentences and all at once, you're reading. "His dog is fat."

TIP 11 The Word Bank.

It is a good idea to make a collection of all the words your child learns to read.

- You will need a box – a shoe-box will do. Write "word bank" on it – use small letters, not capitals. If your child feels like it, he can draw on some barred windows and a door with a large padlock. This is where you are going to keep the words he has learnt to read.

- Find some small white cards to write the words on.

- Make sure you write very clearly – handwriting can be hard for beginner readers.

- Are there any words your child can read already? Write each one on a white card and pop it in the bank.

- Now arrange the wooden or plastic letters in a line on the table in the order of the alphabet. You are going to help your child to read some very simple words.

- Choose a familiar word like "cat". Pick out the letters, put them in front of him, and sound them out with him – **c-a-t**. Next you must teach your child that words have patterns, so that he can collect **word families**.

TIP 12 This is very important. I call it five for the price of one. If you can read *c-at* then you can read *f-at*, and *h-at* and *s-at* and *m-at* and *p-at*. From *s-am* you can make *h-am* and *j-am* and *d-am* and *r-am*.

Every time you make a new word, take the new letter from the alphabet line-up and put the old one back in its right place.

Every time your child learns to read a word, write it on a card and put it in his Word Bank. They will soon add up to quite a few. Even if you only do one word family a day, that will still give you five or more new words each day, and you will soon have 100 words in the Bank. Try *s-it*, *p-it*, *f-it*, *b-it*, *l-it*, or *in*, *b-in*, *f-in*, *p-in*, *t-in*.

Your child is getting words at a cheap price if he learns them in groups like this.

19

I once explained to a man of 30 I was teaching that you could learn to read and spell words in groups. He put his head on the table and started to sob. "Why did no one tell me this when I was seven?" he asked. "I've learnt every word as if it stood alone and it's taken me 30 years to get where I am."

Soon you can start putting two consonants in front of the vowel – *clip*, *spit*, *blot*. Lots more for the Bank.

However, words with no meaning are no use to anyone. So every time your child learns a new word, **discuss its meaning**. This is very, very important. A "fin" is what a fish uses to swim. A "sin" is something you do wrong. "Din" is a loud noise. Your "chin" is under your mouth. This way, you will not only be helping his reading but you will be helping the development of his speech and language too.

TIP 13 Remember to revise the words in the Bank every now and then to make sure he can still work them out. Don't worry if he can't – just keep going over them. He will get there.

Motivation, rewards and bribes

Rewards and bribes can work well, especially for younger children. Smaller goals along the way get small rewards – ten Smarties for ten words, for instance, or a small amount of cash. When your child has 100 words in the Bank, give him a larger reward – a meal out, a film or shopping trip, an extra bedtime story, 15 minutes of extra playtime, or a special DVD to watch. Make a big thing of it. He is on his way to being a reader.

Your child may drive a hard bargain with you. Ben was struggling with his reading. He made a deal with his mum. He would get 1p if he read one page. But she would double his money for every page he read. So if he read two pages, he would get 2p, and if he managed 3 pages it would be 4p. To his mother's surprise he read 15 pages. He only stopped because he had finished the book. Maths was not his mum's strong point. She was amazed when he pointed out with a wicked grin that she owed him £163.84, enough to buy a brilliant new bike. Don't fall for this one!

TIP 14 The tasks you set must not be too hard. If he can't do something, however much he tries, then he will just get upset.

TIP 15 If you take your child out as a reward, try to make sure there are only two in the party. Your child should be the important one. The last thing he wants is two adults talking over his head, or brothers and sisters demanding attention.

Barney, a dyslexic boy of 8, was moving on to another school. He was rather shy and would never read aloud. His mother was concerned that the teacher might be cross. "What can I give you to get you to read aloud to me?" she asked him. "A whole day alone with you, just me and you," was his reply.

Go on adding words to the Bank until your child has started on books. There will come a day, much later, when there are so many words in the Bank that you can't keep track of them all. Bin them with pride. They have done their job.

Words are not just in books

While your child is at the stage when he is just learning to read simple words, you will find plenty to practise on as you go about your everyday life. Words like "car park", "exit", "bus stop" on a trip. "Push" and "pull" on a door. "On" and "off" in the kitchen. Or "lift" and "sports" in a store.

TIP 16 When you go to the supermarket, send him off on his own to find "eggs", "butter" and "flour". And then, best of all, if you have time, go home and bake a cake! When you go to a large store, let him work out where the toy department is and take you there.

TIP 17 Leave notes for him at home. On the kitchen table: "Back at 6 to play footie with you in the park." On his pillow: "You are a star and I love you lots and lots."

TIP 18 When you go out for a meal, encourage your child to read the menu. If it is self-service, give him the money to buy his own food. Words like "fish" and "chips" will soon become familiar. And you've got some more entries for the Word Bank.

Learning longer words

Soon your child will want to read longer words. These can be broken down into units, or syllables. And each of these syllables will have at least one vowel in it!

"Stand" has one syllable.

"Un-der" has two syllables.

"Un-der-stand" has three syllables.

"Mis-un-der-stand" has four syllables.

Each syllable is, on its own, quite easy to read. But how can you tell how many syllables there are in a word?

TIP 19 An easy way to work out syllables. Some people think this is a mystery. But here is a simple trick for you and your child to try. Put one hand firmly under your chin. When you say a word, your chin will come down once for each syllable. Say "seal". Your chin comes down once, so "seal" has one syllable. "Ti-ger" has two syllables. "Chim-pan-zee" has three syllables. "Rhi-no-cer-os" has four syllables. This will also be useful for spelling.

TIP 20 Now you can start adding longer words to the Bank. "In-to", "car-pet", "mar-ket", "sis-ter", "pa-per". There are lots and lots of words that can easily be worked out, once you understand how letters are put together into units and then built up into words.

Learning more difficult words

Unfortunately you can't work out all words as easily as this.

Over 90 per cent of words in the English language obey the "rules" and fit into a pattern.

The rest are tricky ones. They have to be learnt as "sight" words, which means that each is a one-off. For example, words like "does", "said", "because", "your", "many", "water", "some", "walk", "what", "who", "once", "Tuesday" and "eight". You cannot sound these words out. Many of these words are very common. A child will need to read them almost from the start.

TIP 21 You already have a Bank. Why not make a Prison, too? This could be a big money box with a lock and key. Difficult words can go in there as prisoners – 20 at a time, at most. When the child can prove that he really knows the word, it can be let out and another "prisoner" can go in.

TIP 22 Try having one or two "words of the week". Have yellow stickies everywhere, on the fridge, on the mirror, on the TV, etc. As your child learns them, stick them round his room. See how long a line of them you can make and set a target – with, of course, a reward.

TIP 23 There are some good games you can play. Write words on cards, each one on two matching cards, and play Snap. Or turn them face down and play Pairs, where you have to turn them up two at a time and try to find the pair that are the same. (Never use more than 12 words at most. Start with fewer.) Or you can play a version of Snakes and Ladders, where you are saved from the snakes if you can read the top card from the pile on the table.

TIP 24 Let your child jump up and down (on a trampoline is good!), shouting out the letters of a hard word – "b-e-c-a-u-s-e".

Step 3: Starting on books

This is when it really starts to be exciting – when your child can start to read books himself.

TIP 25 Does your child have a bookcase in his room? Give him a bookshelf of his own. Don't wait till he's reading fluently – even if he can't read at all, you can use it for the books you read to him. Put on the shelf books that you love to read together, and books he can read to himself. Don't put on any books that he finds boring, or that are long and difficult. This shelf should celebrate the fun of books.

First books should be easy and well-written. I think Richard Scarry is terrific for little ones. Get children to read aloud with you, to feel comfortable having books around. Get books from charity shops which sell them as cheap as chips; give a book every Christmas and birthday, so that they are recognised as treats and Good Things. Don't rule out Enid Blyton, who has started more people reading for pleasure than anyone else.

Joanna Lumley

TIP 26 Sit beside him while he reads an easy book. Use the five-finger rule. Put a finger on each word that is too hard for him. If you find more than five

27

hard words on on page then the book is too difficult.

TIP 27 Let him point to the words as he reads them. If one is too hard, he should pause, and then you tell him the word. *Do not* say, "You can work that one out," or, "We've had that word several times already." It will stop him in his tracks and he will forget what the sentence is about. Just give him the word. The important thing at this stage is that he should understand the *meaning* of what he is reading, and go fast enough to make sense of the text.

Making his own book

This is a great thing to do. It's much easier if you have access to a computer and can download pictures. You and your child can make something he'll be proud of, using nice materials and taking lots of care. And you can both have fun doing it together. Use simple words, as few as possible, and practise reading them with him.

TIP 28 Once your child starts reading simple books, help him to make a book of his own. Not just a few scraps of paper, but sheets of A4 in a smart ring binder. Let him make a bright cover for it. Put in a few stories or jokes you have shared (typed and printed out if possible). Include his own pictures, with a few speech bubbles that he can fill in and then read back to you. Stick in some holiday snaps or postcards or snippets from the newspaper. Let him write a line or two on every page.

Take a bit of trouble, so he will be keen to show it to other people. Encourage him to take it into school, and if possible warn the teacher first so he or she can make a fuss of him.

TIP 29 Let him tell a simple story for you to write down (in very clear writing) or type into the computer. Give him the page, or print it out. Then let him read it back to you. It will be much easier for him to remember a story he has written himself. Get him to draw some pictures to go with it. Show it off!

Making it fun

Remember that all the activities in this chapter should be fun for both you and your child. You should both feel you are getting somewhere!

TIP 30 One of the best tricks is to get your child to teach you or someone else what he has learnt. It could be your partner, a friend, grandmother or grandfather, a younger brother or sister. Let him give you and others tests and see if he can spot your (perhaps deliberate) mistakes. He will enjoy telling you that you have got it wrong!

TIP 31 Keep on reading to him the books you both enjoy, even if he can read them by himself. Read funny ones so you can laugh together.

TIP 32 Be sure your child practises reading as often as possible. Ten minutes every day is much, much better than an hour once a week.

Susan was nine and could not yet read. Her mother went to their old Irish doctor in despair. "Don't you worry," he said, "or lose a wink of sleep. She's going to get there in the end. And then you are going to be more thrilled and more proud than you ever were with your other children, who have no difficulties to overcome." He was right.

Chapter Two

How Does My Child's Mind Work?

If children are having problems learning to read, it does not mean that they are less clever than the other boys and girls in the class. It doesn't mean that they are lazy either. It may be that their minds just work differently, so they don't respond to the style of teaching that is fine for most of the others.

This chapter looks at ways to understand your child's type of intelligence so that you can find out how to work with it, rather than against it.

Formal Testing

IQ or Wechsler tests

Most children never have a formal intelligence test or IQ test. (IQ stands for Intelligence Quotient, or level of intelligence. Everyone calls it IQ.) People mostly judge how clever children are by their class work, school reports and exam results. But sometimes, if a child is having a lot of problems with reading and school work, he or she will be assessed by an educational psychologist and given an IQ test or Wechsler test. See the appendix (p.128) for how this test works.

This kind of test doesn't predict a child's success in life. Think of brains like cars. Some people have "Rolls-Royce" brains but are bad drivers, so don't get to where they want to be. They do not work hard or make the most of what they have got. Others learn to drive an old banger of a brain with such skill that they will travel a long way.

What you must remember is that tests flag up both the weaknesses and the strengths of your child. They are useful because they suggest the best way to teach him or her, by making the most of strengths and giving support in the areas where he or she has problems.

If your child has formal tests like this, and if you don't understand the psychologist's report, get someone from your child's school to explain it to you. It is well worth the hard work of grasping what is in it, because it will give you a lot of information about your child.

Every child will have a different pattern of difficulty. Every brain is unique. Having a formal assessment may explain why your child finds it hard to learn to read.

Testing reading skills

All children are given tests at regular intervals to see how well they are reading. These record the child's actual age and his or her current level of reading ability. Children are tested on accuracy (how many mistakes they make reading the text) and on comprehension (how well they understand it and can answer questions about it).

These tests compare your child's reading skills with those of an average child of the same age, and from this it's possible to work out his or her formal **"reading age"**. So if Jane is 10 and has a reading age of 12 she will be two years ahead of the average child. If Pete is 10 and has a reading age of 8 he will be two years behind.

By the time you have a reading age of 12 you can read most things. On some tests the highest 'score' you can get is 13. You can cope at university with a reading age of 11. So the task of catching up is not endless! Some tabloid newspapers have a reading age of 9 or 10. But with a reading age of less than 8, a child will find it hard to cope at secondary school.

This is one way teachers will judge how much progress your child is making. They will also want to know what kinds of mistakes he or she is making. Is there a pattern?

TIP 33 You can ask your child's teacher about his or her reading age. It is useful to know when you are buying or borrowing books for them to read.

Getting to know your child – other sorts of intelligence

In 1983 Howard Gardner published a book called *Frames of Mind*. In it he said that there were several kinds of intelligence. Many of these are not assessed by the formal tests.

We are all strong in some areas and weak in others. I am going to describe eight kinds of intelligence and you can work out how they apply to your child. For fun, you can also work out how they relate to your own strengths and weaknesses.

How does this link up to reading?

Well, first, you need to boost your child's self-esteem by finding where his or her talents lie. Confidence in one area will spill over into others. And then you can use their skills and interests to prove how important reading is, if they are to make the most of their talents.

Eight sorts of intelligence

Here are eight areas where your child may have special skills that you can help him or her to develop. Exploring these areas will help both children and adults to make the most of their talents.

1) Skill with words

This is the skill that is so useful at school, and the one that weak readers often lack. These children make jokes and tell stories. They think in words and write lists in their heads. They love word games. They will do well at school because most teachers are skilled with words too, and use spoken and written language all through the day.

All children need help from their parents to develop this skill, because it is so important all through our lives. The advice in this book is to help you do just that.

2) Skill with numbers

These children can work out numbers in their heads. They can remember numbers. They enjoy number games. They will do well in maths class.

You may have to watch out that children with reading difficulties or who don't have English as a first language can understand the "language" of maths. Phrases like "the difference between" or "the sum of" can be quite confusing.

3) Skill at logic

These children like to plan their lives. They love computers, puzzles, Sudoku or chess. They want law and order and will probably plan their time well. They are fond of collecting things like dinosaurs or Warhammer models or stamps.

Often these children want to be organised but don't know where to start. Why not let your child organise your desk or kitchen drawers? He or she may even have a bit of fun afterwards checking up that you are keeping them tidy. Encourage your child to use the computer and to explain to you how it works. If you can, teach him or her words that are useful for computing.

4) Skill at music

These children understand and enjoy music. They can remember melodies and sing in tune.

Children with reading difficulties may find it hard to read music, just as they find it hard to read words. The music teacher may tell you your child is having problems reading the notes. He may also tell you that your child plays by ear, and that is a real gift. But this must not stop him or her from learning to read the notes, however hard that is. These children may have difficulties with the "language" of music, even words like "higher" and "lower" for notes, as they look at the flat piano keyboard. Explain the words to them.

5) Skill at art and design

These children think in 3-D (three dimensions). They build great models. They create pictures in their heads. They take good photos. When they hear a story, they run it as a film in their heads.

Children with reading difficulties may need parents to read the instructions to them if they are to make more complex models. They need help with the hard words. See that your child has lots of paints, felt pens and paper, and display his or her work in your home. Get a photo album and encourage your child to write captions and read them back. Show his or her work proudly to friends and family.

6) Skill with people

These children are good team players. They are able to understand and respect other people. They like working in a group and are interested in what others are doing.

To encourage this skill, read fiction to children so they can learn to relate to the characters. Explain the moods and feelings of other people so they can understand them better.

7) Skill at understanding themselves

These children are independent and like to work alone and think things out for themselves. They know and understand themselves, and what they want and need.

If these children have reading difficulties, parents must make sure their problems do not get overlooked just because they do not share them with anyone.

8) Skill with movement

These children may be good at acting, or dancing, or sport. They know where their bodies are in space and can control their movements.

Children with reading difficulties will need to read to get the most out of their talents and interests in this area. For example, the keen actor may have problems with reading the lines of a play. You could record his drama part on tape. The football-crazy girl may be in trouble because she can't read the sports bulletins on the notice-board. Explain her problem to the staff.

Who am I?

I used to enjoy sorting out with my students what kind of people we all were (yes, me too). It made for good group discussion and we all learned a lot. I worked out that I was good at language and logic, and no good at maths and music.

Thinking about these eight different skills also begins to answer the question, "What type of person is my child?"

If you know who you are, you can judge where you want to get to. And, whatever your target, reading skills are bound to help you on your way.

I spent my childhood reading science books. Now I write novels and poetry and screenplays. It doesn't matter what kids read. What matters is that they discover some passionate interest. In football. In Tudor history. In model planes. In Hogwarts. In chemistry... Give them books about their favourite subject and they'll read. They could be cookery books. They could be car manuals. They could be sports biographies.

It's easy to think that reading is "a good thing". It's not. It's a tool. Kids are not stupid. If you tell them reading is good for them they'll see right through you. They need to know what reading can do. They need to know the doors it can open.

Mark Haddon, author

Life skills

When I was Principal of a school for children with SpLD, including reading problems, I was at first puzzled that their parents reported that their children were having difficulties in the playground, as well as in class. It seemed odd that children would pick on someone just because he was the worst reader in the class. After all, reading is not that cool.

Typical concerns among the parents were:

- Why does my child like to play by himself?
- Why does she shut herself in her room with her iPod and computer when she gets home?
- Why doesn't he understand teasing?
- Why does she get angry or sulky when there are a lot of people about?
- He comes home from school and says the teacher was cross with him and he doesn't know why.

The answer may be just that you have that sort of child. Some children are not "skilled with people" (see number 6 in the list of the different skills). They may find them puzzling and difficult and their moods hard to understand. They may feel happier and safer on their own.

Mark describes how dyslexia affected his time at school.

"I realised that dyslexia was something people chose to believe in or not. I would only tell teachers about my problem if I believed they would be sympathetic. Sometimes I got it wrong and told people who didn't believe in dyslexia that I was dyslexic – this would end in me feeling like a liar, or that the doctor who had told me I was dyslexic had lied to me.

"Being big and gentle, I was mentally bullied by pupils in the higher classes. Some teachers got frustrated with me and would put me down in front of the class, and this would result in more bullying. In the end I started to fight back, which turned me into a bully.

"In the end I sorted myself out and got good GCSEs because of the support of some good teachers. But the biggest help was my parents' support."

TIP 34 Respect the fact that some children want to be alone, and don't nag. They are worn out when they come home from school. Leave them in peace.

TIP 35 If you are going to discuss anything about school with your child, do it over a drink and a snack. No one is at their best if they are thirsty and their tummy is rumbling.

However, it is also true that children with reading problems can often also have social problems. Why is this?

Most of these children have language difficulties generally. They search for the right word when they are speaking, and have to think hard about what is being said to them. They are so busy concentrating on this that they may not pick up on social signals like tone of voice, facial expression and body language. They may not see that the person they are talking to is angry, or tired, or sad, or bored, or joking. And they may not send out the right social signals themselves. So they misunderstand people, and people misunderstand them. Others do not pick on them because they cannot read, but because they are not tracking on the same wave-length.

TIP 36 You can teach children to understand others better by doing some "people-watching" with them, either in real life or on TV. You can also discuss the characters in the books you read together.

- What are the people over there in the cafe talking about?
- Why is the woman so sad?
- Why is that man on the TV programme cross?
- Why does the hero feel so angry at the end of the book?

It was a hot afternoon. Mel and her three sisters wanted to go swimming. "No," said Mum. "I have to wait in for the man to fix the washing machine."

The children went out to play in the garden. But Mel kept coming back in. "Why can't we go swimming?" she asked again and again. At last Mum lost her temper. "Because I say so!" she shouted.

"It's always me you pick on," cried Mel in tears. She was dyslexic/SpLD. The other children realised Mum was fed up, but Mel simply didn't see this.

44

Discuss situations with children which do not involve them and where they are on safe ground, and then you will not confuse them, or hurt their feelings. Help them to read your mind and your partner's. Then they can judge what sort of mood you're in. And don't get too serious. Treat it all as a bit of a game.

Remember, while you are finding out how your child's mind works, it might be useful for him or her to find out a little bit about how your mind works. Show your child that you have strengths and weaknesses too.

TIP 37 One of the best things to boost self-confidence is to help someone else. If your child can read a map for you, or show you how to work your mobile, or mend your bike, you will both get the feel-good factor. And after all, families are for life, and the day will come when your child will take you by the elbow to see you across the road!

If you can make your child more confident and secure, he or she will build up the courage and energy to overcome reading difficulties.

Chapter Three

Types of Reading Problem

Reading is a complex skill. So reading problems may have all sorts of different causes. It is important to be aware of things going on in your child's life that may make it harder for him or her to learn.

Life can be tough!

Lots of things could be happening that make it harder for your child to learn. If any of these are true for your child, extra help may be needed.

- Has he or she been off sick and missed out on a lot of school?

- Has he or she started at a new school? Many children hate change. They have to make new friends and adapt to a new teacher and a new school's teaching style. This is hard work and can slow down their learning.

- Do you speak English at home? If you don't, your child won't be learning as many new English words as his friends.

- Do you read at home? Children copy their parents. If you never pick up a book, then your child is less likely to read. (See p.65.)

- Do you chat to your children, and listen to them? Speaking and listening are important skills that we all have to learn. If parents don't talk a lot to their children, they might be slower to pick up language skills. (See Chapter Four for more on this.)

- When is your child's birthday? In England and Wales, if it's in late summer, he or she will always be one of the youngest in the class because the cut-off point for each school year is August 31st. In Scotland, kids with February birthdays are youngest. That might mean your child is not as developed as his classmates, finds the same work harder, or gets tired more easily.

- Your child may not like the teacher. Children who don't may not make an effort to do well. If the teacher doesn't understand about reading problems, that can be very difficult.

Children can catch up – but the sooner you spot the problem and do something about it, the better.

Miles away...

One common reason for children to fall behind in their reading is that other things in their life are distracting them.

You need concentration to learn to read. Most children only pay attention for part of the time in lessons. I asked a class of 11-year-olds to shut their eyes and stop thinking for five minutes. "We can't!" they cried. When the five minutes were up, I asked them how many had a secret world in their mind that they visited during class time. "How did you know?" they asked.

A lot of children miss out on what is being said in class because they are thinking about other things. In particular it can be very hard for a child who is upset about something. He sits there in the classroom, but does not take in what is going on. His mind is miles away.

So, is your child worrying about something?

- Have there been any dramas in the family? Death or divorce or serious illness will upset children very much.
- Do you or your partner work away a lot? Are you stressed out? Is a brother or sister going through a hard time?
- Is there a new baby coming?
- Do you know or suspect that your child is being bullied?

If your child has any of these problems, you must make sure the school knows. He or she may need extra help and guidance. It will be a bonus to have a teacher who is sympathetic. You don't want the teacher to be cross with the child for not trying, when he or she is upset already.

A few children have **depression**. They are not just upset with good reason but remain in a constant state of gloom whatever is happening around them. This can even happen to very young children, at primary school. A depressed child will not care about praise or blame, and will simply fail to make progress.

This needs to be sorted out by the experts. Talk to the school or your family doctor.

Physical causes of reading problems

Some children have physical problems that make it hard for them to read, no matter how much they try. These children may need to be referred to experts. Here are some of these problems.

Problems with hearing words

Many children who have reading problems at school had hearing problems as infants. They may have had ear infections, like glue ear, and have been partly deaf at times.

If you can't hear properly, it's hard to remember spoken words, and your own speech may be unclear. And when children with hearing problems start learning to read, it's much harder for them to remember how words sound.

This matters because, in reading, one of the skills you need is to recognise words when you sound them out from the letters on the page – and to recognise them fast. To do this, you have to draw on your "memory bank" of sounds you have already heard. If there are too many gaps in your memory bank, or if you have not got the words quite right, it will be hard to read fluently.

If your child has not stored the sounds of words accurately, he or she may not speak clearly. This can be a sign of problems with hearing. But children start to speak at very different ages, so don't start to worry too early. When they start is not so important. How quickly they make progress is important. If your child has, or has had, hearing problems, or if your child's speech is really hard to understand, you may need help from a **speech and language therapist**. First of all, you may want to talk to your doctor.

Problems with seeing words

Some children have problems with seeing the words in front of them clearly. And it's not the same thing as being short-sighted. The letters jump about and change places. These children cannot track a line of print across the page. They lose their place and tire quickly. They may have a "lazy" eye.

Children with these difficulties may not recognise a word when they see it a second or a third time, so you have to tell them over and over again what it is. Don't despair. They will get it in the end. But they will take much longer than their classmates.

Children who tire quickly when they are reading may be sensitive to strong or bright light. Black print on white paper may hurt their eyes. (See p.105 for an idea to help this, and p.134 for information on publishers who print on off-white paper.)

This child may need to see an orthoptist for special tests. Ask your family doctor to refer you to one if you think your child has this sort of problem.

SpLD (Specific Learning Difficulties)

Children who have learning difficulties in some areas are often described as having Specific Learning Difficulties or SpLDs. These children have difficulty in one or more areas of learning, but not all aspects of learning are affected. If children are described as having Learning Difficulties, they have problems with all aspects of learning. So the word "specific" is very important!

SpLD is a name that experts give to some types of learning problems. It is called an "umbrella" term because it covers a wide range of difficulties. Of course, no one child has all of them. It is possible for most children to improve their reading skills, no matter what difficulties they have, but the first step is to understand what those problems are.

The term SpLD includes **dyslexia**, **dyspraxia** and **ADHD**.

Dyslexia

Dyslexia is one of the most common causes of reading difficulties. As many as one child in ten may be affected by dyslexia. Dyslexia may run in families.

The word "dyslexia" is from Greek and means "difficulty with words". But children with dyslexia do not just find it hard to learn to read. They can have one or more of a whole range of problems with writing, spelling, maths, memory and organisation.

Trevor is dyslexic. Here he describes the way his mind works.

"At primary school I could not read, so I would look at comics and compose my own stories based on the pictures. I would turn parts of the playground into rooms and places in my adventure and freely move from place to place talking in the voice of the character. Playground noise was totally lost, as was the bell at the end of play.

"In secondary school, the story-making changed to recalling the important points from the last lesson and explaining to the other pupils what we had just done in science or history. I understood what we had been taught in this type of subject but could only express the answer verbally. I would explain the lesson to the rest of the class in break time. Sadly, it was little use to me, as I still couldn't master written English or Maths, though I could answer the questions others floundered on.

"I still use this gift to design things in my mind and build things without any plans. The whole project is clear like a dream in my mind, and can be retained for years before I turn it into reality. I have spoken to a number of dyslexic engineers who have this gift."

I asked a boy of 11 to tell me what it felt like to be dyslexic. He replied, "Dyslexia's like when the wind blows a television aerial round and the screen goes all fuzzy. My brain is the TV."

We know that the reading difficulties caused by dyslexia have something to do with the way dyslexic people's minds work. Brain scans back up the idea that dyslexic people actually think differently. And because their brains are not wired up the same way as other people's, they need to be taught in a different way.

Dyslexia has nothing to do with being stupid or clever. Some people with dyslexia have great intelligence and talents. If dyslexia is seen as a challenge, not a problem, and if the right teaching methods are used, dyslexic children often do very well in life. Famous dyslexics include Sir Richard Branson, Tom Cruise, Jamie Oliver, Albert Einstein, Walt Disney and Sir Steve Redgrave.

Dyslexic children may need to be referred to a **specialist teacher** or **educational psychologist** for tests (see Chapter Two). Parents should be able to get a dyslexia assessment for the child through school. **The British Dyslexia Association** can tell you how to ask for this. They can also tell you about support in your area. If you cannot have your child assessed through the school, it is possible to have it done privately, but this can be very expensive. You could also ask your doctor.

Dyspraxia

Dyspraxia is a difficulty with planning and co-ordinating movement. A dyspraxic child may have several problems. Terrible handwriting can be one. They may have poor motor skills (movement), can't sit straight, eat very slowly, bump into things and knock things over.

Many of the possible problems do not relate to reading, but there are a few that do:

- Stuttering or unclear speech when reading aloud.
- Losing their place in the text.

- Tiring quickly when reading silently or aloud.

- Finding it hard to remember events that happened in a story in the right order.

- Sitting still to read – they may have to be propped up comfortably.

There are exercises that can improve motor skills and balance. Dyspraxic children can be assessed and helped by an expert **occupational therapist** who has the skills to diagnose and treat this disorder. Contact the **Dyspraxia Foundation** for more advice (see p.133).

ADHD (Attention Deficit Hyperactivity Disorder)

"Why does my child never sit still for two minutes?"

"He roars round the house all day and drives us all mad."

"She distracts everyone else in class."

"He can't concentrate and he doesn't listen."

Your child might have ADHD (Attention Deficit Hyperactivity Disorder). Just like dyslexia and dyspraxia, this is a recognised problem. Discuss it with the school and with your doctor.

ADHD can cause problems with reading. A child with ADHD

- will find it very hard to concentrate
- won't remember the plot
- won't listen to others reading
- won't settle for long

Medication sometimes helps but must be closely supervised by a doctor. It is important to know that the child cannot control his or her restless and unruly behaviour and is not just being naughty.

Contact ADDISS, the National Attention Deficit Disorder Information and Support Service for advice (see p.133).

Keeping track of your child's problems and progress

No one is going to expect you to work out the answers to your child's problems for yourself, or expect you to be able to say exactly what they are. There are experts in school who will do this for you. But you can help them by giving them information about your child's reading habits and attitude to books at home. Keep a record of his or her current level of ability and progress with reading. Talk about your child's feelings, too. Is he or she getting depressed about school? This will help you and the experts to identify the pattern of difficulties that is causing the problem.

A **ring binder** with dividers is a good way to keep a record. (If you find writing difficult, get a friend to help, or write very short notes, and don't worry about spelling as long as you can read it! This is just to help you remember.)

- On a regular basis – say, once a month – describe your child's current difficulties with reading and give a few examples of words he or she can and can't read.

- Write down something about your child's attitude to school. Include any worries he or she may have.

- If you can, photocopy a page of the current reading book from school and underline the words that are too hard for your child to read.

- Is your child's reading improving? Is he or she reading more words? Can you and your child write down some good new words together?

- Write down your concerns and those of anyone else who is close to your child – perhaps your partner or the child's grandparents.

This will be a big help in talking to your child's teacher. You will feel more confident if you have notes to show the teacher. You can also make a list of things you want to ask. When the teacher says, "Why are you worried?" you can use the ring binder to explain.

Take notes of what the teacher says and put them in the ring binder too. If you find writing difficult, it can be really hard to listen and write at the same time. So it's sensible to go to any meeting at school with someone who can write notes for you.

If the school, you and your child are all working as a team, you are going to start to go places. In the next chapters you'll find some tips to get you going. But...

Don't worry too soon!

Try not to panic if your child is learning to read at a different pace from the other children in class. As long as he or she is making progress, that's OK. Children develop at different speeds and young children all make mistakes with their reading. Sometimes, too, parents or teachers just don't ask the right questions.

The teacher showed six-year-old Charlie a picture of a dinosaur and asked him what sound it began with. He said, "It begins with a b." The teacher reported that he was confusing b and d, and that he should be checked for problems.

His mum asked him why he'd said "dinosaur" began with b. Charlie replied, "It was a brachiosaurus."

Chapter Four

Changing Attitudes

This chapter talks about children with reading difficulties, but many of the tips are helpful for all children!

Is your child's reading problem getting you down?

Do you and your child groan when reading is mentioned? There are a whole lot of things you can do before your child gets started on reading to get him or her (and you) in the right mood.

In this chapter you will find tips about how you can change your child's attitude to reading. You can also find tips on re-organising your lives so your child is fit, fresh, and able to put plenty of energy into the hard task ahead.

Choose some of the tips in this book that you think will help you and your child, and get started!

Letting go of your own stress

Difficulty with reading is a very common problem. "Scandal of illiterate 11-year-olds," reads the headline in one English newspaper. "One in seven school-leavers cannot read," says another. "Right now in the US there are almost three million students in special classes because they cannot read," reports an American magazine.

TIP 38 If you are the parent of a child with a reading difficulty, remember you are not alone! Relax and talk about your concerns with other people. There is nothing to be ashamed of.

The first thing you must do is to **stop worrying** that your child can't read. This may sound hard, but if you worry about children, they will start to worry about themselves, and this will destroy their self-confidence.

TIP 39 Find a way to relate to your child's experience. Did you or your partner have problems learning to read? Do you have a brother or sister who is struggling? Or there may be uncles and aunts and cousins with the same difficulties.

If the cause of the problem is dyslexia (see Chapter Three), this often runs in families. If you had similar problems, you will know just what your child is going through. What helped you in the past? Talk to your child about it.

TIP 40 Think about all the things your child can do – sport, music, art, model-making, acting – and talk about how well he or she does them. Take a real interest. See Chapter Two for more about this.

TIP 41 Start to feel good about your child's reading. Convince yourself, and him, that it may take some time, but he *will* get there. Tell him that, when he does learn to read, you're going to be very proud of him.

Setting a good example

How are you going to persuade your child to read books if he or she thinks the computer, TV, Game Boy, iPod or football are more interesting and more fun?

First you must be convinced that reading is exciting. Reading is escape! Reading is cool! Anyone who can't read is missing out!

TIP 42 Be a role model. If you don't read, why should your kids? Let your child see you taking an interest in books. It doesn't matter if it's fact, fiction or a car manual!

My mother was an avid reader who visited the public library several times a week. I would borrow one of her borrowed books from time to time. They were made all the more attractive by the fact that my Uncle Peter banned his wife from reading such lewd material!

Roger Moore

TIP 43 Let your child see you reading at regular times. Sit down and read a book or magazine after dinner. It is much more likely that your child will pick up a book or a comic if you are reading in the same room.

TIP 44 When you read the newspaper, discuss it with your child. Do you share an interest in the sports pages? Do you like reading out bits of news? Could you set aside time for this?

TIP 45 Do your other children read books at home? Might an older brother or sister enjoy reading a popular book out loud?

TIP 46 Make sure your home has books around. Some homes just have a few cookery books in the kitchen. Other homes have shelves of tempting books. It's like faddy eaters. If you want to tempt someone with no appetite then you must have something really tasty to offer. So start collecting a few books for your child that he or she (and you) could really enjoy. It needn't cost a lot – try charity shops, and use your local library. You will find tips on how to choose books in Chapter Six.

Enjoy reading aloud

Dyslexic people and other poor readers do not just have a problem with reading words. They have difficulty understanding what they mean. We don't use all that many words in everyday speech. There are a lot more unfamiliar ones in books. How are children going to get to know them if they can't read?

Well, they will learn new words when you are reading to them. Nearly half of all parents read aloud to their children. And research has shown that children whose parents read to them learn to read faster.

If you aren't a confident reader, this may seem very hard. See pp.70-1 for ideas that can help. Remember, even if you find it hard, your child will love the special time with you.

TIP 47 Have a regular time each day when you read to your child. If possible, choose books he or she can't yet read alone. In term time, this may have to be at bedtime.

TIP 48 Do you skip pages to get to the end faster? Do you and your partner argue with each other over who should read the bedtime story, thinking of it as a chore and a bore? Remember that enthusiasm is catching, and that sharing a story or joke is fun. Instead of groaning that you are tired, let your child see you enjoy the story. Could you compete with your partner for who will read tonight's story? Make it fun for you too!

TIP 49 Have a regular place to read aloud together. This could be in bed, or curled up on a sofa in the sitting room, or outdoors in summer. One girl wanted to read on the stairs. A favourite snack helps to make it feel special.

TIP 50 Let your child choose the book. Even if it's not to your taste, try it out anyway and find out what he or she sees in it.

TIP 51 If your child finds a book boring, let him or her say so. Discuss why the child feels that way.

TIP 52 Be prepared to read the same book more than once. A poor reader is often a poor listener, and will get more out of the book each time. But make sure it's worth reading in the first place!

TIP 53 Explain any words your child doesn't understand. And don't get cross if he or she asks about the same word over and over again. Poor memory is common among less able readers. Have patience and your child will learn it in the end.

TIP 54 Discuss the plot and the characters and the pictures. Encourage your child to re-tell the story to you.

TIP 55 Never push it for too long. As soon as the child tires, or his or her attention wanders, stop. It is best to start with a short session and build it up over time. The aim in the end is to have the child begging for more.

TIP 56 Start as young as possible. Every small child loves a picture book. Start the book habit very young by looking at one together every evening. Get your child used to the idea that the words on the page have meaning, and that they help him or her to enjoy the pictures even more.

TIP 57 If you can't read to your child every night, borrow or buy some story CDs. Most children like to hear the same one over and over again. The Famous Five books, *The Lion, the Witch and the Wardrobe*, Harry Potter stories and *The Hobbit* are all popular. You or your partner or a grandparent could record a very favourite book onto a tape or MP3 player for your child to play when you aren't there, or are cooking or busy with the other children.

Your aim is to get your child listening to words, understanding words and enjoying words. That can open up whole new worlds in stories and books, all just waiting to be explored.

Parents with reading difficulties

There are about seven million people in Britain who can't read very well. So there are many parents who feel unable to help their children much, because they find reading hard. However, this need not be as big a problem as it seems.

- Can you find someone else in the family, such as grandparents, who can read to your child?

- Can you find an older girl or boy who would come a few times a week to read aloud to your child? Offer a small reward, to make sure he or she turns up!

- Get a friend to read one of your child's favourite stories with you until you know it off by heart. You can then "read" it to your child at bedtime. This works well with very simple stories for younger children.

• Borrow audio books from the library and listen with your child. If you look at the words in the matching book at the same time, you will soon begin to work out some of the common words. You can build on that.

• Calibre Audio Library (see p.134) has a free lending service for people with dyslexia or sight problems.

• Listening Books (see p.134) lend out audio books for people who find reading difficult. There is a fee, but some people can get free membership if they can't afford it.

Audio books will teach you and your child lots of interesting new words. You will also get used to the way language is used in books. Written language is a bit different from everyday spoken language. And you will discover which authors you like.

Remember, even if you don't read well, you can learn together. Your child will really love the special time alone with you.

You can make it feel as if you are exploring an exciting new skill! Many adults learn to read properly for the first time by learning alongside their child.

Having someone you love read to you encourages a child's desire to read to themselves. I was never read to. With my own children I read to them long after they'd learnt to read just so we could share closeness and a story. With eleven grandchildren I'm a dead cert to read to them anywhere, anytime.

Dr Miriam Stoppard

Diet, bedtimes, parties and rows!

You are probably wondering what reading has to do with food, or bedtimes, or getting tired or upset. Well, it has lots to do with these things, because you need concentration to read. If your child is to be bright, alert and ready to go through the long school day, you are going to have to make his life easier in other ways.

TIP 58 Make sure children have a good breakfast. Otherwise, halfway through the morning, their energy for work will start to fade. If reading is a problem, your child is going to have to work even harder than the rest, and will need the right fuel in his or her tank.

TIP 59 Make sure that your child doesn't go to bed too late. Save staying up for Fridays and Saturdays when there is no school next morning.

TIP 60 Don't let children go to too many clubs or parties after school on Mondays to Thursdays. They will be bouncing off the wall when they get back. Next day they will be tired and mentally "off work".

TIP 61 Don't have rows with your child before school.

Every day Anna and her mum arrived on the school doorstep screaming at each other. Later on in the reading lesson, I could see Anna fuming with fury at the back of the class. And of course she wasn't hearing a word I said. We sorted it out, the three of us, and it made so much difference.

Getting organised

Children, most of all those with any sort of SpLD (Specific Learning Difficulty), need to arrive in good time for school. If they miss out on the first ten minutes, they will never catch up. The last thing you want for a child with any sort of problem is for them to arrive at school late, or with the wrong gear, or stressed.

As a parent, you can do a lot to see that this doesn't happen.

TIP 62 For a calm start to the day, try to have everything organised the night before. Children who have problems with words find it hard to make lists in their heads. They do not remember what they have to take to school. Don't start the day rushing around looking for things. It's bad for everyone and no one will be in the mood for work later on.

- If you can, pack the school bag and put it by the front door with the jackets or coats. Check that the reading book, pencil case and so on have all gone in. Is there something special your child wants to take to "show and tell"?

- Lay out the clothes for the next day, then you won't be looking for that lost trainer five minutes after you should have left.

- Put the (clean!) lunch box on the kitchen table ready to fill in the morning.

- Put up a notice board in your child's bedroom. Pin up a reminder sheet. Monday – swimming, Tuesday – spellings, Wednesday – football...

- Check in your child's bag for notes or letters that he or she may have forgotten to give you. Do you need to supply tinned food for harvest festival, or an empty jam jar to grow a bean for science?

- Plan ahead. ("Where's my football kit?" "It's in the wash." "But I need it today!")

This way, in the morning, you can concentrate on the essentials – getting children dressed, proper breakfast, teeth brushed – then the kids just pick up their school bags and off they go.

The importance of support

The most important thing to remember is that your child's teacher has him or her for a year, but you have your child for life. You are the ones who know your children best, who understand them, and most of all who love them.

The children whose parents are right behind them with encouragement and practical support are very often the ones who succeed.

Chapter Five

Tots to Teens

> This chapter talks about children with reading difficulties but many of the tips are helpful for all parents!

Reading isn't a skill that exists on its own. It links up with lots of other things going on at different stages of a child's life.

This chapter looks at ways you can help children at each stage of their school life, and even begin preparing them before they start school.

Many of the tips in this chapter are helpful for teaching all children to organise their learning and their lives. They are most important for those children with reading difficulties.

Almost all children who have a hard time with reading will have other Specific Learning Difficulties (SpLDs) as well. These can include difficulties with writing, spelling, maths, memory, organisation, homework or concentration. Later on, it may be with note-taking, revision and exams.

Rob was an only child. He seemed to be a bright and happy little boy before he went to school. He learned to walk and talk in the usual way. He enjoyed making models and doing jigsaws, and he was very good at them. He could switch on the TV when he was two. He loved all the activities at nursery school, the cooking and water play in particular.

But when he started at primary school, something began to go badly wrong. He did not seem able to remember the letters they were learning, and when the others started to read he was left behind. Because reading is the key to so much at school, the gap between Rob and his friends grew wider and wider. Rob became unsettled and began to hate school. He had a tummy ache almost every morning. Sometimes he was even sick on the way to school. He lived for Saturdays and Sundays and the holidays.

His mum was afraid that his teacher and the other children thought Rob was stupid. She had to admit, even she sometimes thought he must be stupid too. But then she looked at the huge and complex Lego fort he had built, at his picture of a goalkeeper flying through the air to head a ball, at his airplane models and Warhammer battle scenes. She heard him explain to his father why the earth went round the sun and why birds migrate. And she knew for sure he wasn't stupid.

Mum realised that there were some big problems that would have to be solved before Rob could use the first-class brain he had been born with.

Rob would be passed from teacher to teacher and go from class to class and school to school. At every stage his mum and dad would have to make sure that everyone understood that this was a boy with talents, but with problems too. They would have to support him and believe in him all through his school years, if he was going to believe in himself. If they did not do this, Rob's confidence would be shattered every time he faced new teachers who did not understand that his brain worked in a different way.

The sooner Rob got help to overcome his reading difficulties, the better.

You do not "grow out" of being dyslexic or having other SpLDs. You just have different problems at different times of your life. But you do learn ways around your difficulties. That's why it's so important to get help early. And why it's so important to talk to your child's teacher if you're worried.

Brett was dyslexic and could not read at the age of nine. Then his parents found a school and a teacher who saw his difficulties as a challenge, not a problem. He started to learn. He passed some GCSEs and even some A-levels. He went to university. Finally he got a job in a bank. At his job interview he told his boss that he was dyslexic, but he also proved that he was a whizz-kid on the computer.

He arrived in plenty of time to catch the London train for his first day at work. Nervous as he was, Brett mis-read the departures board. He got on a non-stop train in the wrong direction, to Oxford. When he finally got to London and to the bank, he was two hours late on his very first day.

The pre-school years

What to look out for

Talk to your child's Early Years Foundation Stage teachers to find out what they think about his or her language development. If there is a history of reading difficulties and dyslexia in your family, you may be watching out for symptoms. Or if you have other children, you may notice that this child is developing rather differently.

Listening and understanding

Children need to listen and understand, and to talk so other people can understand them.

The more children learn to listen, the more they will learn at school.

The more children develop good, clear speech, the better they will get on with other children.

Your aim at this stage is to help your child to understand and use the spoken word. In doing so you will be preparing your child for the much harder task of mastering the written word.

Give them a good start! It may take time and effort on your part, but this will pay off later on.

TIP 63 Giving children your time and total attention as often as possible is one of the most important things you can do. If you do not listen to them, why should they listen to you?

TIP 64 Listen to children carefully. If they make mistakes, for instance saying "efelant" as they point to a picture in a book, say, "Yes, that's an elephant," prompting rather than correcting them. It doesn't help if you use baby language and repeat "efelant". It will just confuse them.

TIP 65 See that they listen to you, and ask them sometimes to repeat what you have just said. Can they remember your exact words? Give a child short messages. "Tell Daddy tea is ready." Praise them when they get it right.

TIP 66 Make instructions very simple, and give them one at a time. Repeat them if the child forgets. "Please go up to your room and fetch your trainers." By the time the child gets to the top of the stairs, the trainers may have gone right out of his or her mind. Don't be cross when he or she comes back without them. Help out and give him or her more of a picture. "Go to your room and get your blue trainers. They're by your bed."

When the messages get a bit more complex, ask the child to repeat them back to you in his or her own words to make sure he has got them right.

TIP 67 Have one friend round to play at a time. If your child is in a group he or she may get left out. Give the children games to play that don't need too much talking – kicking a football around, cooking, painting or making Lego models. Better still, if you can, take the two of them out to the park, or to a cafe for an ice cream. Don't expect your child just to sit and chat to the visitor, as this may lead to confusion, boredom and rows. Play games with them if they don't seem to be getting on.

Stories, songs and rhymes

As well as listening and speaking, the more your child understands about language, the easier it will be for him or her to learn to read.

TIP 68 Read to your child a little at a time and ask questions to make sure he or she has understood. Even better, get the child to ask you the questions. Stop if he or she gets bored. Reading should be fun! See Chapter Four for more on reading aloud and bedtime stories.

TIP 69 Tell your child short stories. Talk about the naughty things you did when you were little. That's always very popular! Then see if he or she can tell the same story to someone else and get it right. Or retell a favourite fairy story.

TIP 70 Read lots of nursery rhymes to help your child recognise the patterns in words – "Little Bo P-eep has lost her sh-eep."

TIP 71 Teach your child short songs – *Twinkle, Twinkle Little Star* or *The Wheels on the Bus*. Sing along at first and then let your child sing them to you. Act them out. It will help him or her to remember them.

Finding the right word

TIP 72 If your child forgets names of objects, and calls them all "things", spend time pointing to pictures in books.

"That's a kettle." Then ask more about it. "What do you use a kettle for? Have we got a kettle at home? What colour is it?" You will be expanding your child's word store and helping him or her to remember the word "kettle".

Most important of all, read to your child every day and let him or her see you reading too.

Primary school

Basic skills in listening, talking, reading and maths are some of the most important things you learn in class at primary school. Writing and spelling matter too, but not so much.

Many children who have problems with reading didn't hear properly when they were younger and starting to talk. They may have had glue ear. (See p.50.) As a result they heard words in a fuzzy kind of way. It must be like hearing messages about train times at the station when the system isn't working well, or listening to a radio that crackles. You have to make a huge effort to make out what is being said, and sometimes you fail.

TIP 73 Always look at your child when you speak to him or her, and speak slowly and clearly. If necessary, pause and wait for your child to catch up.

Later on, when your child is trying to "sound out" the words in a book, he or she will find it hard to blend the different sounds of the letters in the right order. They may say "par cark" instead of "car park". They may leave out bits of words, and say "rember" for "remember".

TIP 74 Write one of the longer words from a school reading book on a strip of card and cut it up: re – mem – ber. Shuffle the pieces and get your child to read each one, and then put the word together again in the right order.

TIP 75 This is important. When you have taught your child something, let him or her try it out on you. Let the child copy down a word, cut it up in bits, and make you put it together again. Have you done it right? He or she must tell you.

I taught all my four children the alphabet by pretending I didn't know it. "I need to learn it so badly," I told them, "to use a dictionary, or look up a name in the phone book." They were cross when they realised later on that I had been pretending. But by that time they knew their alphabet by heart.

TIP 76 Play listening games with your children. Puppets are fun. Make them tell jokes, sing songs, tease each other and tell each other stories. Get your child to pretend that a puppet is reading the book. Any mistakes the puppet makes are its own, not your child's. Get the child to teach the puppet to count or how to read simple words.

TIP 77 If you can, keep in close touch with the teacher. If possible, for example, find out in the first year which letter or letters the children are doing each week and use them at home. Then play games with the letter. How many names can you think of beginning with J? James, Jane, Jack, Jaspreet, Jenny, Jitender, Josh, Jess, Jamal, Joe, Jaden...

TIP 78 Be careful not to blame the teacher (or the child or yourself!) if progress in reading is slow. Be really pleased each time you notice that your child has made a step forward, even if it is only a small one. It's nice to write a

note to the teacher to tell him or her so.
And talk to the teacher too to find out
how best you can help.

Teens and secondary school

Children who can't read by the time they
transfer to secondary school will be bored
and frustrated in class. Every day of their
school life they will be made to feel stupid.
Or lazy. Or both. There is a real risk that
the bored non-reader will opt out, or bunk
off and get into trouble.

For children who have found reading
hard early on, it may always be quite slow.
And it is likely to be only one of a number
of difficulties.

These days, however, much more is being
done about poor readers at secondary level.
There is more help on offer than there used
to be. It is still important for you to find
out how your child is being helped at
school and to go on talking to the teachers
about what you can do at home to support
them.

There are still many ways that parents
can help, too, though with teenagers you
will have to be much, much more tactful.

You will probably not be able to "teach" your teenager much at this stage, because mums and dads are not cool any more. But you can help in other ways.

TIP 79 At secondary school, your child will have several different teachers. Make sure that they all know about his or her problems. Get in touch with the form teacher or tutor if you have to, or even the head teacher. Let your child's teachers know if there is a real overload on homework and if he or she is failing to complete it, or taking far too long.

Smoothing the path

Because learning is hard for them, children with reading problems will get more tired than others and will only be able to focus on their work for shorter periods. Smooth out your child's life generally and he or she will have more time to concentrate on reading.

TIP 80 For any job, it is helpful to have the right tools.

- Make sure your children have all the pads, pens, pencils, rubbers, ring binders and folders that they need.

- Post-it notes, coloured dividers, index cards and highlighters will help them to organise   their work.

- Make sure they are working in a good light and the room is not too hot or too cold. Many teenagers don't notice this!

- See that they have a good, clear dictionary and a thesaurus (both with pictures if possible). A thesaurus lists words that are similar to one another, so if you look up "naughty" you will find "unruly", "wild", "cheeky", "badly behaved" and so on. This is a good way to learn new words.

- Make sure each child has a watch (digital is best) with a face that is easy to read. That will help them to organise their lives.

- If you have one, give them access to a computer at home to research school work. Best of all, let them have their own. Or encourage them to use one in the local library. If at all possible, see that they learn to touch-type.

Joanna had a holiday task. She had a book on the Wars of the Roses to read and 50 questions to answer.

The teacher knew Joanna had problems. So she marked beside each question the page in the book where the answer could be found.

Joanna answered all the questions. She only got five wrong.

"So who was fighting who?" I asked her.

"I never discovered," she replied.

Struggling readers often see only the parts, not the whole.

Helping with homework

TIP 81 Arrange a place where children can do homework without being disturbed. If possible it should be somewhere away from the TV and family chat, where they can really concentrate.

TIP 82 If your child will let you, read his or her lesson notes and see if they make sense. If they don't, consult with the teacher.

TIP 83 Find out what topics the class are doing at school that term. Suggest that you go to the library together and see if they have any books on those subjects that are simply written, with pictures if possible.

TIP 84 If your child is studying a book or play, see if he or she would like to get a CD or DVD of it to listen to or watch at home.

TIP 85 SpLD children may not be able to read their own writing. Buddy up with another mum or dad. If your child has forgotten what the homework is, or if what's written down doesn't make sense, ring the other parent and ask.

Make your child more independent

When your child is a teenager, it's even more important that they don't see you are worried about them.

Treat them as young adults. Discuss family plans with them and take their advice sometimes. Let them be private when they want to be. Knock on their bedroom door when you want to go in.

TIP 86 Behave as if you are certain that SpLD children can sort things out for themselves – and make sure that, in fact, your child can.

- They need to be able to read the local bus and train timetable.
- Make sure they can deal with money.
- They may find it hard to remember phone messages or be slow to write t them down. Give them some ideas to help. "The line is very bad, could you repeat that please," they could say.

Teenagers can be moody and difficult, but they can also be great fun. Dyslexic children often have original minds and great ideas – having one in the family can be a big bonus.

If, that is, you can accept them just as they are!

Chapter Six

Choosing the Right Book

Start with what you love!

Children who have made a great effort to learn to read need books that will reward them. Exciting books. Fun books. Interesting books. Both fact and fiction should be an escape into a different world, a voyage of discovery.

Children like to feel that they become friends with the authors of the books they read. This way, reading is never a lonely exercise. It helps to get to know an author you like, and then read several of his or her books. How many readers have got going on Enid Blyton's Secret Seven or Famous Five series? The reader becomes familiar with the characters, the setting, the vocabulary and the style. This makes it easier to master the text and to follow the story.

TIP 87 Find an author your child likes and then get more books by the same writer. Try children's authors that all children love. Terry Deary, Michael

Morpurgo, Hilary McKay and Jacqueline Wilson are all popular. Then your child will feel that he or she is just like the others in class.

I know as an adult that it sometimes requires a great deal of mental energy to start a new book. "Who are all these people? Why should I care about any of them? What's going on? What's on the telly?" That's why series books are so popular. The reader knows where they stand when they start.

It's the same with kids. A new book can be very daunting. Get them started by reading it to them, if they're hooked, let them take over. If not, then dump it (there's no shame in that) and try something else – anything else! In the end you'll find something that clicks and then, take it from me, you'll really miss the nights spent reading to them.

Charlie Higson

Graded Readers

"Pat and the pig trip and crash into a big box."

This is easy to read, but who cares?

"The sack must have a duck in it."

What does it matter?

Both these examples come from standard "graded reading" books. The child may be able to read every word, but why bother?

"Graded readers" are series of books which start easy and get slowly harder. They have their place in the early stages of learning to read. Some are better than others, but very few of them are "real" books by well-known authors. And they are almost all written for younger children.

Children with difficulties are often given graded readers for far longer than their class-mates. Too long, in fact. This is not what most of the class are reading. The children feel patronised and can get very, very bored. "I hate reading," they say, and hide their books.

I was always a passionate reader as a kid – with a torch under the bedclothes, all that sort of thing – and I was anxious to pass that on to my children. So I always read to them, and it was a joy when you could see they were really engaged in something. The problem I found was that, when they started reading for themselves, the stories had to be so much simpler that I couldn't get them motivated. I've still not worked out a way round that.

Adrian Chiles

How can children take pride in learning to read, or believe that you can read for pleasure, if they get so little reward for so much effort?

As soon as readers have even a small degree of fluency, they need to move on to "real" books. In the meantime it helps a lot if parents and carers can read to them the kind of books they really enjoy.

Dave was at a school for children with SpLD. His sister, Emily, who was two years younger, was reading fluently at age six. She loved books.

Dave was 11 and still struggling. It had taken two years of intensive help to get him to a reading age of 8 (see p.33). Now it was a real problem to find anything that he could read that was not too childish. The books for his age were too long, the words too hard, the print too small. He would read a few pages, close the book, and say, "Reading is for girls."

Real books for struggling readers

As a teacher, I complained for many years that children who found reading difficult had their biggest problem when they were ready to start on "real" books. The ones they could read were too childish. The books they wanted to read were too long and difficult.

When I retired from teaching, 10 years ago, I helped to set up a publishing company, Barrington Stoke, to publish books that were what these children wanted. They had to be short, with gripping plots and interesting characters. They had to be written by authors that other kids in the same class were reading. They had to be easy to read – so we chose letter shapes that helped dyslexics, and used yellow or off-white paper so that readers' eyes didn't get so tired. The covers had to look good.

And every word had to be checked by less confident readers, who told us if they had any problems reading and understanding the text. They also told us if the conversations sounded like real children or teenagers, and if they got bored or fed up with the stories! All Barrington Stoke books are still checked by children before publication to make sure they are exactly what readers want.

Many publishers now produce the tempting books by well-known authors that these children need. You should be able to find books that are right for your child's age and interests, but that he or she can read without too much difficulty.

How to find the right books

It is helpful to know your child's "reading age" (see p.33). Some publishers describe their books as for "teenagers with a reading age of 7" or "10–14-year-olds with a reading age of 8". Others will simply say that their books are for struggling or less able readers.

Your school library should have "high-interest, low reading age" books. Ask the librarian for help. A good bookshop or local library can also help you find what you need (see p.112).

You can buy books on line through the publisher's website, or through Amazon.co.uk. Or phone the publisher and ask for a catalogue.

You can find a huge amount of information online.

- www.booktrust.co.uk and www.readingzone.com have lots of reviews, many by children.
- www.lovereading4kids.co.uk, and www.wordpool.co.uk have sections on books for reluctant readers.
- The National Literacy Trust, www.literacytrust.org.uk, has lots of useful advice and articles.

Publishers and book series to ask for

Madeleine Lindley Ltd select the best children's books for primary and secondary classrooms. I asked them to recommend some publishers and series for reluctant and struggling readers. There are other good publishers and series, but this list gives you a place to start.

The list on the next page gives the publisher, the name of the series, the kind of books in the series, and the publishers' suggestions for the series' reading age and "interest age" (the actual age of the children who may like these books).

	Type of book	Reading age	Interest age
Badger Publishing			
First Flight	Fiction, poetry and non-fiction	6 to 6.5	7 to 12
Full Flight: Runway	Fiction	6	7 to 14
Full Flight	Fiction, poetry and non-fiction	7.5 to 8	8 to 12
Rex Jones	Fiction	6.5 to 7	8 to 14
Dark Flight	Fiction	6.5 to 7	10 to 14
Barrington Stoke			
Younger Fiction	Fiction	8	9 to 12
Teen Fiction	Fiction	8	Teen
Reloaded	Myths and legends	8	10 to 14
Reality Check	Non-fiction	8	10 to 14
FYI	Fiction with facts	8	10 to 14
Gr8reads	Fiction	7	Teen
Solo	Fiction	6.5	10 to 14
Go!	Fiction and non-fiction	6	11 to 14
Ransom Publishing			
Boffin Boy	Manga-style comic books	6 to 7	8 to 14
Trailblazer	Fiction and non-fiction	6 to 7	8 to 14
Siti's Sisters	Fiction (aimed at girls)	7 to 8	10 to 14
Dark Man	Fiction	5 to 8	Teen to young adult
Watts			
Fast Lane	Fiction	6 to 8	13 to 15
I Hero	Interactive adventure series	7 to 9	7 to 12
Wayland			
Tremors	Fiction	8 to 10	9 to 12
A&C Black			
Colour Graffix	Graphic novels	7	9 to 14

Choosing a book

What should you look for when you choose a book for your child?

There is no secret, magic book that all children love and want to read, kept in a special locked room in a magic bookshop. You might think it's a shame that there isn't. How it would make things easier. The thing about books, though, is that we all like different ones, and thank God for that, or the rest of us writers might just as well give up.

I could list my top ten choices, but they wouldn't work for everybody. I've lost count of the times that friends have given my kids books for their birthdays, saying, "Oh, mine all loved this," only to find that my own kids have no interest at all in it. I can hardly bear to mention the number of copies of *Swallows and Amazons* given by elderly relatives that stand gathering dust in the corner – the books, not the relatives. "Oh, I loved these stories when I was your age." Forget it. My only advice would be – don't give them *Swallows and Amazons*, they'll be bored to tears.

Charlie Higson

TIP 88 When you pick a book, think about how you and your child are going to read it. That will help you decide how hard or easy the book can be. Are you going to:

- Read the book to your child?

- Read the book together?

- Expect your child to read the book to himself or herself? If this is the case, then remember, KISS – Keep It Short and Simple.

The look of the book

First impressions are very important.

TIP 89 Look at the cover. It should look cool. It should tempt the reader. It should not say anywhere on it that it is for "less able" readers. Does it look girly, or is it clearly for boys? Many boys won't look at a book in a pink cover, girls may love them! What does the title tell you?

TIP 90 Read the "blurb" on the back – this is a short piece that tells you what the book is about.

You know your child. Is this the kind of book he or she likes? It's no good buying a book on football if your son hates sport.

Your daughter may want adventure, not 'girly' books. And some children find horror stories give them nightmares.

Is the main character a boy or a girl? That's worth thinking about when you're choosing for either sex.

Is the story dramatic, or fun, or scary? The blurb on this one sounds good for a child who likes horror or ghost stories, not so good for someone who wants lots of jokes!

Screams in the night.

Shadows in the moonlight.

The Vampire of Croglin is the whisper on everyone's lips.

But is there a darker secret?

One boy is about to find out...

(*The Vampire of Croglin* by Terry Deary)

TIP 91 Look at the print. The "font", or style of the print, should be clear – nothing fancy. As one child put it, "I don't like it when the 'f's and the 's's look like squashed house flies." The size of the print should not be too small or cramped. It must not be too dense, either, and the text should be well spaced out on the page.

Print that is too large is harder to read, because you can only see one or two words at a time. To become a fluent reader you need to read the text in chunks, four or five words at a time. It is then much easier to grasp the meaning.

TIP 92 Print that is very black on very white paper can hurt sensitive eyes. If this is a problem, but this is exactly the book your child wants to read, put a transparent, coloured sheet over the page to cut out the glare (see p.133). Let the child pick which colour they prefer. Books printed on off white or cream paper can also help.

TIP 93 When you choose a book make sure that the pictures appeal to your child. Pictures should not be too "busy" but should clearly make a point. Just as it helps if a book is by a first-class author, a first-class illustrator is important too. Childish or silly pictures, or ones that are not cool, will put off the reluctant reader.

Pictures are very helpful in fiction for the less able reader.

- They can help the child find his or her place.

- They can explain a difficult word.

- They break up the text and make it more friendly.

- They can help children with any sort of reading difficulty to remember the plot, as they can flick back through the pictures to remind themselves what happened.

- They can help the reader to identify the characters and settings so the text can get on and tell the story.

Often there are no pictures in fiction intended for children over eight. However, there are lots of pictures in books of facts. Publishers like Usborne, Dorling Kindersley and Kingfisher publish non-fiction with lots of pictures on all kinds of topics.

The language and style of the book

Less able readers often have a small vocabulary. You can't really read a word if you don't know its meaning. So it may be possible to work out what words like "lethal" or "flinch" or "subtle" sound like, but this is not much good if you don't know what they mean.

If children can create a picture of the word in their mind, it is easier to read. So they can read "binoculars" or "millionaire" or even "paranoid" (they say all their mums are paranoid). But they do not like words like "usually" or "probably" or "intently" (all adverbs), which do not link to any image in their brain.

Here's an example of how the less confident reader may tackle a word.

"I don't understand the word 'intently'. Could 'intently' be the opposite of 'tently'? Has it got something to do with tents? If I try taking off the 'ly', it says 'intent'. What on earth does that mean? Oh, I give up."

Very long words are difficult, as the struggling reader has to stop to work them out and forgets what the rest of the sentence is all about.

TIP 94 Flick through the book and see how many hard words you can find. More than five on one page is too many. Even when the words are short, a text can be hard to read if the sense is not clear. For instance "I am as I am". The words are simple but it is not easy to puzzle out.

Jokes and puns may need explaining.

TIP 95 Explain any joke you come across in a book, and then get your child to retell it to someone.

If the book is for teenagers, and most of all if it is written in the first person – the "I" of the story – then the language should relate to the way young adults actually think and speak.

"I hate it when girls cry. I find it really embarrassing," were the words in the text. But "embarrassing" is a hard word. "That's not a word we use anyway," said Chris. "It would have been much better if he'd said, 'I hate it when girls cry. It makes me want to puke.'"

Figures of speech and many common expressions can be hard too.

Mark was reading a book where the hero "pushed his glasses up his nose". Mark was puzzled. "How could he see out of them after that?"

If you want to feel like a child with a language problem, try talking without using any word with an "m" in it. This will really slow you down and you will soon get in a muddle remembering what you wanted to say. It's like this for many struggling readers most of the time.

Find out about the story

When you pick up a book, see if you get gripped when you sample a page or two of it. Read the first and last page. So much is about confidence and interest. A child who is excited by the story may amaze you by reading words you expect him to give up on.

TIP 96 Make sure there is plenty of action. The less able reader will remember the story not by retelling it, but by running it like a film in his head. Encourage children to do this if it helps them, as remembering the story in words can be tricky for children with SpLD.

Flashbacks are tricky. Some stories jump about a lot in time. This is very hard for the poor reader. It is best to stick to stories that have a simple beginning, middle and end.

Here's Jade describing the book she has just read with me. She talks in a low, flat voice and very fast. If you have read the book you can understand exactly what Jade is saying. If not, she will seem rather confused.

"Well there was this guy see and his mum had something wrong with her see and yes she'd had an accident and it was a car accident and she'd been badly hurt see and this guy was really upset and yes she was going to die see and he couldn't talk to his dad but they got together and decided to kill her off."

Fact or fiction?

So far we have been looking mostly at fiction. But many of the points I have made about language and lay-out apply to factual books too.

It is sometimes said that boys respond better to fact than fiction. But for thousands of years people have loved to hear a good story, well told. It is an escape and an adventure. We lose ourselves in another world. One of the joys of reading fiction is that we find characters who think as we do. They become friends.

Children who can't or don't want to read stories miss out on a lot.

TIP 97 A collection of short stories can be useful, as it looks like a full-length book but the content is divided into easily manageable sections.

Where to get books

Bookshops

Bookshops can be quite alarming places.

James went into a bookshop and asked at the information counter where he would find a book on chess.

"Go up the stairs at the back of the shop and turn right at the top. You'll find yourself in the History section. Go through there and on through Philosophy and Gardening and turn left. You will see the section on Games on the further wall."

James was dyslexic and found it hard to remember instructions. He walked out of the shop.

The answer is to find a smaller bookshop with an assistant who knows something about reading difficulties. Your local Dyslexia Association branch could help you with this.

Libraries

This is a very good option. If librarians are not too busy, they will often come over and help you find the book you want. If you go often enough, they will get to know you and begin to suggest books you might like.

There is the huge advantage that you can return the book if it is the wrong one.

The Internet

The great advantage here is that the computer is so very private. You can surf around a site like Amazon.co.uk (who sell every sort of book) on screen in your own home and not feel that people are watching you and noticing that you are choosing easy options. Amazon even notes what you like and offers you similar books – personal service!

TIP 98 Give children some money of their own just to buy books. It could be in the form of a book token, then you know they can't spend it on anything else! Persuade them to think that reading a book is a treat.

Reading doesn't always mean books

It takes time to read a book – especially for struggling readers. But there are plenty of other enjoyable materials out there which will help your child improve his or her reading skills.

A quick flick through a **magazine** is a great way to get some reading in. There are plenty of magazines for fans of football, films or computer games. Celebrity magazines are often popular.

Comics are fine, but they are often hard to read because the text is in capitals. Words in capitals are hard because they are unfamiliar and have little shape. Compare "elephant", which is up-down-up in shape, with "ELEPHANT", which is uniform. Another problem with comics is that it can be confusing working out the order of the cartoons on a page. However, graphic novels can really appeal to children who resist books, and can get them into the habit of reading.

The **Internet** has created a new sort of reading. Children who have little time for books will spend hours glued to the computer screen. But at least there is some involvement with words, and reading skills are needed to find favourite sites. Even if the contact with words is scrappy, there is at least the possibility of choice and inter-action. It is not like watching TV, which is a passive way to pass the time and demands no input from the viewer. If exploring the web improves reading skills, then it may encourage children to open a book.

Your child may like looking at anything from car manuals to catalogues. It's all reading material, so if the child is interested, encourage it – and as he or she builds up better reading skills, maybe you can find books on the subject too.

I came from a working family where books weren't available, but when I went to school I discovered the now often derided

Janet and John series and realised that the black marks on paper could give me access to other worlds. I was thrilled. Please, don't be worried by your children's initial choice of books, just encourage them to read and they'll soon widen their horizons – exactly as I did.

Gilda O'Neill, bestselling historian and novelist

Happy reading!

Chapter Seven

Adults and Reading

There are two reasons why this short chapter is needed.

- Your child will grow up one day.
- You or your partner may have a reading difficulty.

There are lots of reasons why adults may not enjoy or feel confident about their own reading. For example, dyslexia and other reading problems often run in families, so it may not only be your child who finds reading really hard. Maybe you do too.

We are told that one in ten children is dyslexic. So one in ten adults must be dyslexic too. And that includes parents and grandparents.

The more help you get as a dyslexic child, the better you will be able to cope with reading as an adult. However, the problems of dyslexia have only been understood in the last few years. So there are a lot of adults out there who had a rotten time at school, because no one knew why they couldn't learn like the others.

About seven million people in this country have real problems with reading. How many of them are parents? Are you one of them? And are you asking yourself how you can help your child to read better?

TIP 99 If you have a lot of problems with reading, then go back to the beginning with your children. You may be surprised to find that you actually know more than you thought, as you read the easy books they start on. You just have to keep one jump ahead.

Unless you get help, reading difficulties don't go away as you grow older. You just find ways to get round them.

For several years I taught young offenders in their late teens. Many of them could not read at all. Nor could their parents. I grew angry that our school system had failed them. No wonder they bunked off class if they could not read. They were frustrated and bored every day of their school life.

One day, late for my class, a young man called Clive rushed in, red in the face. "Cook just called me an illiterate bastard," he said. "And I think illiterate is a really dirty word!"

Was it Clive's fault he could not read?

With regular lessons and the right teaching these young adults all learnt to read. It was just sad that they had to commit a crime before they got this chance. One day they would be fathers. What chance would they have of helping their own children if they could not read themselves?

Adult learning

I have taught many adults to read. It can be an exciting process and it can transform someone's life. Learning as an adult is not like going to school. You are free to choose when and where you learn, and how you'd like to go about it. You and your teacher work together, as equals.

TIP 100 Think about why you want to improve your reading. It's usually much easier to stick with a plan if you know what you want to achieve. Lots of parents decide to work on their own reading skills so that they can help their children.

Adults have different reading needs

Some people can read a bit but are just slow to work out the words, so they miss the meaning. This may mean they give up. They may want to concentrate on a few chosen areas.

Terry was a taxi driver. He needed to read the names of streets and houses. So we practised working out what words said, without bothering too much about their meaning. He also wanted to read to his little girl, who had just started school. So he came to me with her favourite books, so that he could learn to read them aloud to her in the evening. And he also wanted to read the racing tips in the newspaper. So we worked on the vocabulary of racing.

Others worry because they know they have off days when they are tired or stressed. This happens in exams, then it's easy to misread the question and give the wrong answer.

George was a geology student at London University. His long-term girl-friend had helped him to get through his A levels. But at the end of his first year at university he crashed badly.

He was tested and found to be very bright – and very dyslexic. We worked on this for the next two years (there is never a quick fix). He learnt to read all the geological terms. I had never heard of many of them and he taught me a lot. His confidence grew and he ended up with a good degree.

Twenty years later he contacted me. He was doing an exam in wine and he still found exams stressful. Could I help him again?

Sometimes there are specific areas of reading people worry about – and they can be important.

Sue was a nurse. She was fantastic with the patients. But she worried all the time about reading medical notes. She needed to become more familiar with the vocabulary of medicine. She had to stop being ashamed of her reading problems. She had to learn to admit them and ask for help.

Again, I learned a lot as we went through the list of words a kind doctor had prepared for us.

Each person and each family develops a different pattern of difficulty. Just as the problems are different, so each one must be solved in a different way.

In the Parker family, mother, son and daughter all really disliked reading aloud, not because they couldn't read but because the sound of their own voice distracted them. If they wanted to enjoy reading as a family the best thing was to listen to an audio book together.

Andrew says: "As a teenager struggling with undiagnosed dyslexia, I battled through my required reading. Throughout my schooling I only read the minimum to get me through. Books were a painful chore, not a pleasure. Other people enjoyed reading. I did not. Other people read books. I did not. Other people discussed books. I did not. They were an embarrassing gap in my life, something to avoid. I simply could not understand how people could read so much, so fast or how they could possibly enjoy it...

"I discovered audio books when I was in my mid-thirties. It was a wonderful experience, an awakening. Reading opens a window on the world of human experiences and frees the soul to dream."

You can learn to read at any age. I have had students aged 50 or older. You can improve your reading at any age. And you can change your children's future for the better by helping them to read, even if you are not a confident reader yourself.

People who can read take it for granted. Those who can't read must be given every chance to learn, so they don't miss out.

Getting help

There are plenty of places you can go to for support and advice. Addresses and contact details are on p.132–5.

If you would like to improve your own reading:

Free classes for adults are run in many places. There are some classes for parents who want to help their children. They are sometimes called "Family Learning".

- Colleges of Further Education. Phone or ask at the information desk for details.
- Surestart centres, Job Centres and community centres. Ask staff for advice.
- Workplaces may run courses. Talk to your manager, someone from Human Resources, or your Union Learning Rep if you have one.

- Libraries often have information about classes to help you work on your reading. Ask for help at the information desk.
- Schools. Talk to teachers at your child's school
- You can also contact Learndirect to find out about classes in your local area. Call 0800 101901 for more information.

If you would like to learn but don't want to attend a class, or find it difficult to get to one, then you can sometimes learn online. Try calling Learndirect or look at BBC Skillswise.

If you are concerned about dyslexia:

The **British Dyslexia Association** and **Dyslexia Action** are both excellent sources of information, as is the **Adult Dyslexia Organisation**. The British Dyslexia Association can tell you about your local dyslexia association.

Talk to your family doctor if you are concerned about your own or your children's dyslexia. They may be able to refer you to someone who can help.

The **Dyslexia Teaching Centre** in London and the **Helen Arkell Centre** in Surrey offer assessments and tutorials. The dyslexia groups mentioned above will be able to tell you about getting help in your local area. You may be able to get help with the cost. For example, the Helen Arkell Centre offers free consultations for people who are out of work, either for themselves or for their children.

Students can seek support at their chosen university. They can apply for extra time in exams, computer hardware and special tuition. They may be eligible to apply for a Disabled Student's Allowance. Dyslexia associations can give you more information on this.

The **Disability Discrimination Act** protects adult dyslexics in the workplace. It's up to you to decide if you want to mention your dyslexia at work. Think about it, and perhaps call the British Dyslexia Association helpline or your local dyslexia group for advice before you take action.

If you want to, you can discuss your dyslexia with your employer or the human resources officer at work. Many employers give financial help for assessment and tuition. Discuss any problems at work arising directly from your dyslexia. Very often there are ways round them.

If you want to discuss your dyslexia, don't forget to mention, for example at a **job interview**, the benefits of dyslexia – the original "thinking outside the box" and the ability to solve a problem by looking at it in a different way. (See pp.54–5.)

Books for less confident adult readers

Several publishers produce good books for adults who find reading hard.

- **Quick Reads** are short, fast-paced books by bestselling writers and celebrities. They are perfect for people looking for an introduction to reading as well as regular readers who want a bite-sized book.

- Barrington Stoke publish a series called **Most Wanted** – short thrillers for adults.

- The **Open Doors** series published in Ireland offers short novels by well-known Irish writers, aimed at adult readers.
- Sandstone Press have the **Vista** series of short, quick reads.

You can find these books in good bookshops or on the Internet.

Finally...

Follow the tips in this book that suit you. Don't give up if it takes time. And remember that everything you do is worth it. You will make a huge difference to your child's reading – and their future – just by spending that special time with them. Enjoy it!

TIP 101 This is the most important tip of all. It is the advice my father gave me.

"It is not what you do for your children, but what you do with your children that counts."

Appendix

Support from schools

Only 20 years ago there was little support in many schools for children with SpLD. Some people did not think there was such a thing as dyslexia. They thought it was an excuse to hide the fact that a child was lazy or stupid.

All this has changed now, and new laws have been passed to make sure that schools give support when and where it is needed.

In 2001 the SEN (Special Educational Needs) Code of Practice was set up. Schools must identify children with "additional" needs and provide them with the extra help they require. They must also keep in close touch with parents, offering them advice and informing them of any support programme that has been set up for their child.

Schools provide IEPs (Individual Education Plans) for children getting extra help. These can be usefully discussed at meetings and parents' evenings. They monitor the child's progress and set out short- and long-term aims.

The Education Act of 1996 established Parent Partnership Services. All schools must ensure that the parents of children with "additional" needs are given the information and advice they require to make decisions and choices about the education of their child.

The Government is aware of the low levels of literacy in this country. They called on Sir Jim Rose to make an independent study of the most effective methods of teaching reading. He produced the Rose Review of Reading. The Government is researching how the teaching of reading can be improved, so that all children, including those with SpLD, will master basic reading skills and have a better chance in life.

The Wechsler Test

The Wechsler Test IV is one that educational psychologists often give. This test has several sub-tests, which look at various areas of thinking skills. They are divided into four groups: Verbal Comprehension, Perceptual Reasoning, Working Memory and Processing Speed.

Verbal Comprehension is all about how children use and understand language. How many words does the child know? Does he understand how words link with each other (such as "carrot" and "cabbage")? How good is his comprehension (understanding) of the world around him?

The **Perceptual Reasoning** sub-tests do not require the child to use words and are sometimes called non-verbal tests. They are all about visual and manual skills. He will be asked to arrange coloured blocks to make patterns, choose pictures that belong together, or make groups of visual patterns or symbols.

The other two sections, **Working Memory** and **Processing Speed**, will highlight children with specific difficulties in these areas. But it is the verbal and perceptual subtests that highlight the higher reading skills of the brain.

The results of these sub-tests will be added up and the child will be given a formal **IQ score**.

A few children do well in all the sub-tests and produce a high score. Many children, of course, score at an average level. Some other children will do very well on some sub-tests and badly on others. These are often the ones with SpLD (Specific Learning Difficulties).

Useful Addresses

Dyslexia and other conditions

Adult Dyslexia Organisation
Ground Floor, Secker House, Minten Road,
London, SW9 7TP
Helpline: 0207 924 9559
Email: dyslexia.hq@dial.pipex.com

British Dyslexia Association
Unit 8, Bracknell Beeches, Old Bracknell Lane,
Bracknell RG12 7BW
Helpline: 0845 251 9002
Email: helpline@bdadyslexia.org.uk
Website: www.bdadyslexia.org.uk

Dyslexia Action
Park House, Wick Road, Egham, Surrey TW20 0HH
Phone: 01784 222300
Email: info@dyslexiaaction.org.uk
Website: www.dyslexiaaction.org.uk

Dyslexia Scotland
Helpline: 0844 800 84 84
Website: www.dyslexiascotland.org.uk

Helen Arkell Dyslexia Centre
Frensham, Farnham, Surrey, GU10 3BW
Phone: 01252 792400
Bookshop: 01252 797511
E-mail: enquiries@arkellcentre.org.uk
Website: www.arkellcentre.org.uk

The Dyslexia Teaching Centre
23 Kensington Square London, W8 5HN
Phone: 020 7361 4790
Email: dyslexiateacher@tiscali.co.uk
Website: www.dyslexiateachingcentre.co.uk

Xtraordinary People
Phone: 0118 929 6948
E-mail: info@xtraordinarypeople.com
Website: www.xtraordinarypeople.com

Dyspraxia Foundation
8 West Alley, Hitchin, Herts, SG5 1EG
Helpline: 01462 454 986
Email: dyspraxia@dyspraxiafoundation.org.uk
Website: www.dyspraxiafoundation.org.uk

Attention Deficit Disorder Information Support Service
Phone: 020 8952 2800,
Website: www.addiss.co.uk

Association For All Speech Impaired Children
Afasic, 20 Bowling Green Lane, London EC1R 0BD
Helpline: 0845 3 55 55 77
Email: info@afasic.org.uk
Website: www.afasic.org.uk

General

Crossbow Education (Coloured overlays)
41 Sawpit Lane, Brocton, Stafford, ST17 0TE
Phone: 01785 660902
Email: sales@crossboweducation.com
Website: www.crossboweducation.com

Audio books

The National Listening Library
Listening Books, 12 Lant St, London SE1 1QH
Phone: 020 7407 9417
Email: info@listening-books.org.uk.
Website: www.listening-books.org.uk

Calibre Audio Library
Aylesbury, Bucks HP22 5XQ
Phone: 01296 432 339
www.calibre.org.uk

Publishers

Barrington Stoke
18 Walker Street, Edinburgh, EH3 7LP
Phone: 0131 225 4113
Email: barrington@barringtonstoke.co.uk
Website: www.barringtonstoke.co.uk

Open Doors (New Island publishers)
2 Brookside
Dundrum Rd
Dublin 14
Phone: 00 353 1 2989937 / 2983411
Website: www.newisland.ie

Quick Reads
The Quick Reads Team, NIACE, Renaissance
House, 20 Princess Road West, Leicester, LE1 6TP
Phone: 0116 204 7072
Email: quickreads@niace.org.uk
Website: www.niace.org.uk/quickreads

Sandstone Press
PO Box 5725, One High Street, Dingwall, Ross-shire, IV15 9WJ
Phone: 01349 862 583
Email:info@sandstonepress.com
Website: www.sandstonepress.com

Book websites

www.booktrust.co.uk
www.literacytrust.org.uk
www.lovereading4kids.co.uk
www.readingzone.com
www.wordpool.co.uk

Adult learning

learndirect
PO Box 900, Leicester, LE1 6ER
Phone: 0800 101 901
Website: www.learndirect.co.uk

NIACE (National Institute of Adult Continuing Education)
Renaissance House, 20 Princess Road West, Leicester, LE1 6TP
Phone: 0116 204 4200
Email: enquiries@niace.org.uk
Website: www.niace.org.uk

NIACE Dysgu Cymru
3rd Floor, 35 Cathedral Road, Cardiff, CF11 9HB, Wales
Phone: 0292 0370900
Email:enquiries@niacedc.org.uk
Website: www.niacedc.org.uk

Quick Reads

Pick up a book today

Quick Reads are bite-sized books by bestselling writers and well-known personalities for people who want a short, fast-paced read. They are designed to be read and enjoyed by avid readers and by people who never had or who have lost the reading habit.

Quick Reads are published alongside and in partnership with BBC RaW.

We would like to thank all our partners in the Quick Reads project for their help and support:

**Arts Council England
The Department for Innovation, Universities and Skills
NIACE
unionlearn
National Book Tokens
The Vital Link
The Reading Agency
National Literacy Trust
Welsh Books Council
Basic Skills Cymru, Welsh Assembly Government
Wales Accent Press
The Big Plus Scotland
DELNI
NALA**

Quick Reads would also like to thank the Department for Innovation, Universities and Skills; Arts Council England and World Book Day for their sponsorship and NIACE for their outreach work.

Quick Reads is a World Book Day initiative.
www.quickreads.org.uk   www.worldbookday.com